BUCKEYE WISDOM
Insight and Inspiration from Coach Earle Bruce

Earle Bruce
Compiled by Lynn Bruce Smith and Bill Rabinowitz

TRIUMPH
B O O K S

© 1999, 2014 by Earle Bruce

All rights reserved.

No part of this publication may be reproduced, stored in a retrieval system, or transmitted, in any form by any means, electronic, mechanical, photocopying, or otherwise, without the prior written consent of the publisher, Triumph Books LLC, 814 North Franklin, Chicago, Illinois 60610.

Printed in the United States of America

This book is available in quantity at special discounts for your group or organization. For more information, contact:

Triumph Books LLC
814 North Franklin
Chicago, Illinois 60610

ISBN: 978-1-60078-852-9

Design by Patricia Frey

Teacher,

When I think of my Grandpa, I think of the word hero.
He is clever and gutsy.
I think of people I look up to, and each of them go back to him.
Chris Spielman, Greg Frey, all go back to him.
He coached them all and they coach me.
I think he is a great coach, and because of that, so are they.
And because of that, I am achieving what I strive for.

By Zach Smith, grandson of Earle Bruce
and wide receivers coach at Ohio State University

Contents

Acknowledgments

Coaching for forty-three years was a lot of fun and very little work. It was the people I associated with that made it that way—assistant coaches, players, secretaries, trainers, equipment people, and all the others connected to the game of football.

In coaching high school teams, I had the opportunity to influence young men and motivate them to much greater heights than they had ever imagined achieving. The quality of high school coaching when I was an assistant and head coach was unbelievable. I was an assistant to Bill Peterson (later head coach at Florida State University and the Houston Oilers) and Bob McNea (later assistant coach at Northwestern and Kent State University). They both taught me about football, relationships with players, and motivation. As a high school coach, I spoke at many football clinics and interacted with many fine high school coaches, namely: Bob Seaman, Sandusky, Massillon, and Worthington High Schools; Pat Mancuso, Leetonia and Princeton High Schools; and Tony Munafo, Huron High School. Bron Bacevich from Cincinnati Roger Bacon, who I affectionately called "Old Man," was a coach who really contributed to my speechmaking and motivational material. What a coach, what a person, what a great human being. He worked at the game and was a fine coach for seventy years at Roger Bacon. His record of 311 victories is only surpassed by his success in the personal relationships he had with his players.

When I arrived at Ohio State University as an assistant coach, I met Glenn "Tiger" Ellison, then a freshman coach. He not only provided me with the "Big John" story, but with many others. He was a master of motivation and success to coaches and all professionals. He was always positive and exciting to be around.

I hope you get the idea that this book reflects many years of being around good people with great written and oral thoughts on football and life. Some thoughts have unknown sources, but are common thoughts-for-the-day. I don't want credit for originality, I only want credit for using such great material for the book.

Thanks for the material and thanks to all the great contributors of this book.

CHAPTER 1

On Winning and Losing

"The game (football) has become the symbol of our country's best qualities . . . courage, stamina, coordinated efficiency. Many believe in these days of doubt and indecision that through this sport we can best keep alive the spirit of reality and enterprise which has made us great. Upon the fields of friendly strife are sown the seeds that, upon other fields, on other days, will bear the fruits of victory."

—General Douglas MacArthur

Success in football is in direct proportion to how your great football players play in the big games–and how your "others" rise to the occasion. Great players always play well in big games and make big plays. They meet the challenge, and then some. Let's all remember that the opponents we play have great players–let's give them credit for their plays. We all recognize great effort, desire, great teamwork, and great coaching during the game. Don't bring up the negative or the adverse plays or criticize individual players or coaches. Remember to criticize the performance, not the performer. Mistakes do happen and they are tough to accept, but mistakes are accentuated more when you lose. The next game is the most important game, not the last game.

~ One Way To Win ~

After a losing game, it is tough to prepare for the next opponent. There is always too much talk about the lost game. But if you really think about winning, there is only "One Way To Win."

It takes a little courage
And a little self control,
And some grim determination
If you want to reach the goal.
It takes a deal of striving,
And a firm and stern set chin,
No matter what the battle
If you really want to win.

There is no easy path to glory,
There's no rosy road to fame.
Football, however we may view it
Is no simple parlor game.
But its prizes call for fighting,
For endurance and for grit,
For a rugged disposition
And a "don't know when to quit."

You must take a blow or give one,
You must risk and you must lose,
And expect that in the struggle
You will suffer from the bruise.
But you mustn't wince or falter,
If the fight you once begin,
Be a man and face the battle
That's the only way to win.

Fans don't win or lose football games. But fan support is very important to a winning college football program. Fans don't make tackles, or blocks, or field goals, or block punts. Fans do motivate players by cheering them to greater heights.

The great football players motivate themselves; they are self-starters. The players must be hitters, have toughness and discipline, and execute assignments for success in football. They must not miss tackles or blocks, show weakness, or make mistakes.

Lessons about football and life are learned on the football field. One lesson is that your own mistakes kill you. The quarterback must learn to take a sack and not throw the ball up for grabs. Sometimes the lesson is listen to what your coach says and have the sense to do what he says. Don't defend someone's poor actions or poor mouth in the game–see to it that concentration on the game and your job in the game gets all of your attention. This is called focus! You lose as a team or win as a team. Good leadership directs a team to victory because you have everyone on the same page.

~ Winning and something even more important ~

When I look back at my career, in most cases if there was an important football game, I can remember most of the good plays and the bad plays and everything about the game. The game was always important to me. That was my profession. But when you have a football team, what lasts even longer than the game results are the relationships. I try to remember the good things players do without remembering any of the bad.

I still cherish being on sidelines during games when I could tell when our team was playing above themselves, giving the greatest effort they could possibly give. That's a rewarding thing. It's still a game of winning and losing, but it's also about learning something from each game you've played – taking things that makes you a better person, a better player, just better.

A good football coach can teach a young man to play football and teach him to play it the right way and really learn something from the game. From that, they can take things from the game that helps them be a better person for our society. It teaches them how to be a tougher person and more caring person and one that knows what teamwork is and success is—and that you get to be successful through hard work and toughness.

~ Winners vs. Losers ~

When a winner makes a mistake, he says "I was wrong,"
  When a loser makes a mistake, he says, "It wasn't my fault."

A winner works harder than a loser and has more time,
  A loser is always too busy to do what is necessary.

A winner makes commitments,
  A loser makes promises.

A winner says, "I am good, but not as good as I ought to be,"
  A loser says, "I'm not as bad as a lot of other people."

A winner listens,
  A loser just waits until it is his turn to talk.

A winner respects those who are superior to him and tries to learn something from them,
  A loser resents those who are superior to him and tries to find chinks in their armor.

A winner feels responsible for more than his job,
  A loser says, "I only work here."

A winner says, "There ought to be a better way to do it,"
  A loser says, "That's the way it's always been done here."

Michigan game, 1998

What a great victory in the "Horseshoe" last Saturday! What a great victory for the players, coaches, and the avid Buckeye fans. What great support for the Buckeyes in their 31-16 victory over archrival Michigan. Winning is very satisfying and it sure makes the winning spirit contagious. The victory was well deserved and the Buckeyes earned it. Let's repeat the reasons for the great victory over Michigan:

> The trenches won the big battle and the war. The offensive and defensive lines dominated Michigan.

> The turnover battle was won 2-1.

> Special teams held the edge over Michigan with a blocked punt and forced bad punts. Good kickoff coverage.

> The Buckeyes' good, big players stepped forward for the "Big Game." Germaine, Boston, Winfield, Katzenmoyer, Miller, Wiley, and Moore all played an outstanding game.

> The state of Ohio was truly "Scarlet & Gray" on Saturday, and, oh yeah, all of Michigan was "Blue."

CHAPTER 2

On Football

"I sometimes wonder whether those of us who love football fully appreciate its great lessons. That dedication, discipline, and teamwork are necessary for success. We take it for granted that the players will spare no sacrifice to become alert, strong, and skilled—that they will give their best on the field. This is as it should be, and we must never expect less, but I am extremely anxious that its implications not be lost on us."

—President John F. Kennedy

E very season, I put down some thoughts about football, the season, people, and life:

Everyone has problems. Solve your problems. Remember, the only people without problems are in cemeteries.

Lead, follow, or get the hell out of the way.

What is, was; what was, is; what will be is up to me.

Others can stop you temporarily, only you can do it permanently.

There are three kinds of people—those who make things happen, those who watch things happen, and those who don't know what the hell happened.

Your goals don't start in your brain, they start in your heart.

Learn to be the rider, not the horse.

Life cannot be like playing out of a sandtrap; it's got to be like sinking the four-foot putt for the win or the championship.

Criticize the performance, not the performer.

Success is the old "ABCs"—Ability, Breaks, Courage.

Pay your fair share. Pay ahead, not back.

Don't be afraid to say, "I don't know" or "I'm sorry."

Let people know what you stand for and what you won't stand for.

Stick your head in the sand and one thing is for sure—you'll get your butt kicked.

There are only two things in life—Reasons and Results. Reasons don't count.

~ The daily football exercises ~

Every football team does daily calisthenics. Here are a few additional exercises to improve your performance:

Football eye exercise—See the perfection in the opponents.

Football tongue exercise—Speak from the heart instead of the mouth.

Football facial exercise—Smile often.

Football hearing exercise—When we speak we learn nothing. Listening is the teacher.

Football brain exercise—Think only constructive thoughts. Good reading is to the mind what exercise is to the body.

Football leg exercise—Walk toward respect for the opponent, wisdom, health, and great sportsmanship.

Football breathing exercise—Inhale the great moments in sports. Exhale spitefulness and all negative thoughts.

Football strength exercise—Have the strength to endure when things go wrong and to win the next game after losing the previous one.

Football heart exercise—Have the heart to constructively improve self, teammates, school, community, and country.

Football soul exercise—We are never alone. Walk with your team and with God.

I have always said that football is the greatest team game. Players have the opportunity to learn the following:

To bounce up when knocked to the ground.

To control tempers in competition.

To give of themselves in an unselfish manner, which binds them in unity with their teammates through teamwork.

To exercise honest judgment and alert thinking and acting accordingly.

To learn that the meaning of discipline is to take orders and carry them out to the best of their ability.

To develop confidence in themselves.

To train themselves with courage and stability in competition.

To arm themselves with patience when discouraged.

To conduct themselves in a grown-up manner.

To overcome fear, envy, worry, revenge, injury, and weather.

That the football field is neutral; it is for all, no matter their race, creed, color, or religion.

It is my contention that to be number one in any sport, especially college football, takes a lot of hard work and sacrifice. There are no easy ways to become number one. You may get away with natural ability or talent, but natural ability will only take you so far. Number one is almost always the person or team that works the hardest.

Along with hard work comes sacrifice. If you really want to be number one, you have to pay the price. You have to practice hard and then spend time watching films of yourself and the opponent. You have to practice when you'd rather be doing something else. Everyone likes to win, but how many want to prepare to win?

Because of your sacrifice, your reward will be greater when you reach your goal. With sacrifice and hard work, you can expect to win, because you will never be defeated the easy way. Sacrifice makes victory sweeter.

Use practice time to build confidence. Do whatever it takes in practice to become a winner. *Success is not spontaneous combustion. You have to set yourself on fire.*

In times when everything is not always clear, we must keep things in perspective. Here are the "Ten Commandments of Football" for the high school or college football player.

1. Thou shalt not quit

2. Thou shalt not have an alibi

3. Thou shalt not gloat over winning

4. Thou shalt not sulk over losing

5. Thou shalt not take unfair advantage

6. Thou shalt not ask of others what thou art unwilling to give of thyself

7. Thou shalt always be willing to give thine opponent courtesy

8. Thou shalt not underestimate an opponent, nor overestimate thyself

9. Remember that the game is the thing; and he who thinks otherwise is no true player

10. Honor the game of football, for he who plays the game straight and hard wins, even when he loses

St. Francis De Sales: *"We shall steer safely through every storm, so long as our heart is right, our intention fervent, our courage steadfast, and our trust fixed in God."*

~ The Company He Chooses ~

Football players are high profile. Players must be cognizant of the places they go, and the people they associate with must be of high caliber.

I learned a foolish little poem when I was an assistant coach at Ohio State that has stuck with me. I have read it at the beginning of the football season to all of my teams.

It was sometime in November
In a town I can't remember
I was carrying home a jag with maudlin pride
When my feet begin to stutter
And I fell down in the gutter
And a pig came up and lay down by my side.

As I lay there in the gutter
Thinking thoughts I dare not utter
A lady passing by was heard to say
"You can tell a man who boozes
by the company he chooses,"
And the pig got up and slowly walked away.

Here is some advice for a successful stretch run in November:

If you work hard, give your best effort, but think that sometimes it is not paying off—*Work hard and give your best effort anyway.*

Honesty and speaking with frankness makes you vulnerable to criticism—*Be honest and speak frankly anyway.*

It is sometimes difficult for players to listen to their parents and coaches because of peer pressure—*Listen to your parents and coaches anyway.*

Winners never make excuses; losers do—*Be a winner.*

When a great player speaks, everyone listens. When a lesser player speaks, not many listen—*Be a great player.*

Fans, media, friends, and enemies are negative, unreasonable, critical, and illogical at times—*Love them anyway.*

To improve your performance in November, improve your attitude—*Attitude is the answer to improvement.*

Say good things about the game of football, your opponents, or your team, and you might get criticized—*Say good things anyway.*

The measure of a good Buckeyes football player is the tape he puts around his heart, not his head—*Be a good Buckeyes football player.*

~ Champions ~

Great emphasis is placed every year on the championship, whether it be a Big Ten Championship or a National Championship. There is only one champion or co-champions. Let's all think about being a champ.

Conditioned for the task supreme,
Confident in coach and team,
Courageous when the going is rough,
Champions never say, "enough."

Heart to meet the game's bad breaks,
Heads to know just what it takes,
Hands that work through thick and thin,
Honest champions play to win.

Ambitious to develop now,
Abilities that God endows,
Aiming high to meet the test,
A champion wants to be the best.

Marked and watched where'er he goes,
Model traits he has to show,
Manliness if in defeat,
Modest in the victor's seat.

Practice, practice, ever on the move,
Plugging daily to improve,
Perfection, that he'll never see,
Peerless champs just try to be.

~ Some thoughts on football and life ~

Real wealth comes to the one who learns that he is paid best for the things he does for nothing.

What lies behind us and what lies before us are tiny matters compared to what lies within us.

To be average is to be the lowest of the good and the best of the bad. Who wants to be average?

Noah didn't wait for his ship to come in—he built one.

Don't look back unless you plan to go that way.

Ideas are funny things—they don't work unless you do.

One cannot always be a hero, but one can be a man.

Have patience—all things are difficult before they become easy.

There is nothing so uncertain as a sure thing.

It is a case of give and take in this world, with not enough people willing to give what it takes.

The test of your football courage comes when you are faced with one of the many rugged goal-line stands forged by the opponent.

~ Things to think about ~

Hey, all you Buckeyes, here are some things to think about:

Fear makes the Wolverine seem bigger than he is.

Birthdays are good for you. Statistics show that the people who have the most birthdays live the longest.

Courage is contagious. When a brave player takes a stand or makes a great play, the other players' spines stiffen and they play better.

Wolverines can stop you temporarily but the Buckeyes are the only ones who can do it permanently.

No Buckeyes coach knows his true character until he has lost to Michigan twice, disciplined a great player, moved his TV show from WBNS, and thumbed his nose at the alumni.

I don't think much of a player who is not better today than he was yesterday.

The greatest pleasure in coaching is winning a game that people think you cannot win.

Example is not the main thing in influencing others, it is the only thing.

A wise man sometimes changes his mind, but a fool never does.

We don't need any more leadership training, we need some followership training.

~ Ten Cannots ~

You cannot bring prosperity by discouraging thrift.

You cannot strengthen the weak by weakening the strong.

You cannot help small men by tearing down big men.

You cannot help the poor by destroying the rich.

You cannot lift the wage earner by pulling down the wage payer.

You cannot keep out of trouble by spending more than your income.

You cannot further brotherhood of men by inciting class hatred.

You cannot establish sound security on borrowed money.

You cannot build character and courage by taking a man's initiative.

You cannot really help men by having the government tax them to do for them what they can and should do for themselves.

—Abraham Lincoln

~ You Just Can't Win ~

I'm not allowed to run the train, or see how fast t'will go,
I ain't allowed to let off steam or make the whistle blow.
I cannot exercise control or even ring the bell,
But let the damn thing jump the track and see who catches hell.

—Malleable Iron Co.

Michigan Game, 1981

I n 1981, at the Friday Booster Luncheon at the Sheraton Inn before the Michigan game, the Booster Club was depressed because of the loss to Minnesota 35-31 two weeks before. *The Football News* had said that Bo could name his score against the Buckeyes. I told the club they would be proud of the Buckeyes versus the Wolverines on Saturday.

We played great defense, limited the Wolverines to three field goals, and gained the lead with 2:50 remaining to make the score 14-9. The defensive secondary was super, limiting Anthony Carter to four catches, fifty-two yards, and zero touchdowns. As always, Marcus Marek played outstandingly with sixteen tackles and one interception; Glen Cobb had fifteen tackles; Anthony Griggs had ten tackles; and Will Foster had eight tackles. As for turnovers, always important in this game for a win, there were three interceptions and one fumble recovery for the Buckeyes.

The offense had two eighty-yard drives to win the game. Tim Spencer had 110 yards in 25 carries and tight end John Frank had 7 catches for 68 yards. Art Schlichter was 12 for 24 for 131 yards. A great four-yard run by Art for the winning touchdown was made possible by an outstanding block on the defensive end by Vaughn Broadnaux.

If you want to beat Michigan, you must shut them down in the 4th quarter and score some Buckeyes points. When you win, you can walk broad and high; if you lose, you go through the alleys of Columbus. This game will always be special to me.

CHAPTER 3

On Assistant Coaching

"Picking an assistant coach, the first thing I was interested in was the man's character."

—Woody Hayes

~ Assistant Coaches ~

God bless good assistant football coaches. Having been an assistant coach as well as a head coach in high school and in college, I really appreciate good assistant coaches. They are not always given the credit they deserve and sometimes are given too much criticism for losses. I have had some very good and successful assistant coaches, and I myself worked for three fine head coaches: Bill Peterson and Bob McNea at Mansfield High School and Woody Hayes at Ohio State University. Four of my former assistant coaches have been head coaches in the National Football League—Joe Bugel, Pete Carroll, Nick Saban, and Dom Capers—and many of my assistants have become head coaches in the college ranks.

Like head coaches, the assistant's job has become a little less time consuming with the changing and shortening of the recruiting season from late May to early February. The assistant's job is a matter of recruiting, coaching, handling players, and showing loyalty to the program and head coach. One duty I learned from Coach Hayes was to help a player get his education and graduate from Ohio State. If you demand effort on the football field, you should aid him in having the same performance in the classroom.

Coach Hayes said, "If you recruit him to play football and you promise him an education in return, then you see to it that he attends class, gets good tutors, attends study table, gets a schedule of classes he can succeed at, and receives his degree in four to five years." When the player has problems off the field or gets lazy in the classroom, a coach must do for him as he would do on the practice field—CARE.

The reason I am an Ohio State graduate is because of Coach Hayes and that philosophy. I'll bet there are a lot more out there like me.

~ My first year with Woody ~

I joined the staff in July 1966 so my first spring practice was the next year. I'm coaching spring ball, and things are going terrible. I go in afterwards to the trainer and the doctor, Dr. Murphy, and head athletic trainer Ernie Biggs and said, "I've got a problem. I've got a tight chest. I feel like it's coming in on me." They said, "Welcome to the club." I said, "What club? What are you talking about?" They said, "The assistant coaches' club at Ohio State. Every assistant coach that's ever come here has come in the first week of spring practice and said, 'I have a tightening or weakness of the chest.' Every one."

I said, "What do you do about it?" They said, "Here's a Valium. You go home and take the Valium an hour before you get into a tub of water about two feet deep. You go in the tub and sit in the tub for about a half-hour or hour – whatever it takes – and just cuss Woody Hayes out until you're done. And then you walk away and you'll walk away and have no more chest pains." I said, "You've got to be kidding me." They said, "We're not kidding you. You better do it. It works." So I go home and tell Jean the story. I got the Valium out and said that I have to take this Valium and go in the tub and cuss him out for an hour. She said, "What?!" and I said, "Yeah, that's what I said." She asked if I was going to do it and I told her that they told me to do it. So I get in the tub and I start cussing him out and I hear my 2-year-old and 4-year-old. They're down on the floor outside the door saying, "Who's in there, Daddy?! Who's in there with you, Daddy?!" They were all worried that their daddy was in trouble.

~ Wives ~

Any coach who's honest will tell you that having a supportive wife is essential. I certainly did with Jean. And a head coach who knows how to get on the good side with an assistant's wife is one smart head coach. Woody certainly did that with Jean.

When I was coaching high school football at Mansfield, I used to come down here a lot for different things. One time Woody invited me to the Memorial Day recruiting session that he had. When I came down, I brought Jean, then my girlfriend, as my date. We walked in and I introduced Jean to coach Hayes. "This is Jean French." I saw her face when she was introduced. She was overwhelmed. I guess he was one of the greatest persons she'd ever been introduced to.

Another time, I came back down and we're walking down the hall and Woody comes out of his office and comes over and says, "Hi, Jean, how are you doing?" We talked awhile and then we went to the car and then she's looking funny. I say, "What the hell's the matter?" She said, "He remembered my name." I said to Jean, "He remembers my name." Then she said, "No, you don't understand. He remembered my name. No one remembers my name. But he did."

So now we're married, and then I go to work for Woody Hayes. When I took the job, I knew I better not bring any bad stories back home. But one night, Woody took this Kodak camera and threw it against the wall, and it stuck in the wall. So I came home and said, "Jean, you know what coach Hayes did tonight? He threw the projector against the wall." She said, "Coach Hayes wouldn't do that." I said that he did. That's what she used to tell me, "Coach Hayes wouldn't do that." She'd been smitten a little bit. But that's the way it is. I always had to back down.

~ Movie Man ~

One of my jobs in my early years under Woody was to be in charge of the movies the team would see the night before a game. Woody didn't go to the movies. He would stay and watch game film instead. All he cared about were two things: The movie had to be done in time for our 9:45 p.m. team meeting, and the movie shouldn't be a comedy or a horror film. Most of the time we went to Disney movies. That's not exactly what college kids want to watch, and finally my group – the centers and guards – said to me before a game at Minnesota in 1969, "If we go to another Disney film, we're going to throw you in that lake out there."

So Woody asked what the movie options were, I said that I don't go to movies, but that the kids wanted to see "Easy Rider." He said, "What do you know about it?" I told him I don't know anything about any movie. I never have time to go to a movie. Then I told him that if we go to another Disney movie, they're going to throw me in the lake and I would like not to be thrown in the lake.

So we come back from the movie and Dave McClain, a first-year defensive-line coach who went on to become Wisconsin's head coach, was the first one off the bus. There stands Woody and Woody asks, "How was the movie?" Dave says, "It's the worst movie I ever saw." I went, ooh, he just stabbed me in the back. He didn't know Woody at all.

We beat Minnesota 34-7, but the Gophers did a good job maintaining possession and holding the score down. That was after we'd won the national title and were scoring 60 points a game. So on Monday morning after looking at the film, Woody kept us waiting for 45 minutes, not saying anything and just staring with his head in his hands and then he said, "I know what it was. It was the damn movie." And I went, "Oh God." It couldn't have hurt more. He said who's in charge of the movies and I said that I was. He said, "You're fired." Fortunately, the firing applied only to being in charge of the movies.

~ Music Man ~

After getting fired from my movie job, I was assigned to be in charge of the music. I kind of delegated that to Rudy Hubbard, who happened to be Ohio State's first black assistant coach, and he brings in music that was a little different than what we had been used to. All of a sudden, it's being played in the locker room and then Woody comes in. He's going berserk. "Turn that goddamn music off! You can't listen to that stuff and play football! You'll be discomboberated." I'm not sure what that word meant, but we got the idea. I knew I had get out of there as fast as I could and snuck out to the john. The next morning, Woody says, "Who's in charge of the music? You're fired. Rudy, you're in charge." All I could do was laugh. But quietly, to myself.

~ Right side of the ball ~

I was there six years. Six years is a long time to be a position coach under coach Hayes. I started as the defensive backfield coach. We weren't blessed with the fastest guys in the defensive secondary. Woody was in charge of the offense and he kept the fastest guys for himself. That was the problem. You never saw Woody if you were a defensive coach. You saw him for 20 or 30 minutes whenever he had a meeting with the whole coaching staff and then he'd say, "OK, you're on your own," and he took over the offense.

~ Brick fantasies ~

It was about my fifth or sixth year, and I started to feel like I had become the most picked-on assistant ever. I started having dreams at home, and I'd think, "Holy crap, this is bad." I thought about getting out of coaching and becoming a fish-and-chips franchisee. I also thought about Wendy's, but I couldn't raise enough money for a franchise. But it was really getting to me. I knew that coach Hayes always came in about 6 or 6:30 in the morning and watched film. I started dreaming of being on top of the football building with a big brick and dropping it on him as he walked in. Can you imagine that? Think about that. But I think some other coaches thought about that, too.

But now when I think back about coach Hayes, my thoughts are so different. He's my No. 1 guy. I'm probably more like him in coaching than anyone else. He's a very successful guy, a very intelligent guy. Twenty-eight years at Ohio State, that's unbelievable. I don't think anyone will last 28 years again, the way things are. He came here in '51. We didn't even get scholarships until '57. Woody Hayes dominated this place for 30 years."

~ The last laugh ~

I attribute my career to one decision made by Woody Hayes. I hurt my knee during my freshman year, ending my career before it started, and I went back home to Cumberland, MD. I didn't know what I was going to do or where I was going to go. Woody Hayes sent someone to get in touch with me to come back and help coach. That saved my life in the sense of what I did then. I came back and did coach. Little did I know that I would be the guy to replace Woody Hayes. When I was in my third year under Bob McNea at Mansfield High School, he asked me what my goal was in coaching. I said, "I want to be the head coach at Ohio State," and we laughed and laughed at laughed. When I got job at Ohio State I called him. I wanted to hire him as my recruiting coordinator. And we thought about that statement I made all those years earlier and we laughed and we laughed and we laughed.

~ Being Woody Hayes' successor ~

After he got fired after the 1978 Gator Bowl and I became head coach, our relationship changed. When I came back, he treated me well. He knew before most people, probably as soon as anybody, that I was getting this job. He told some of my friends about it. He was excellent to me. He didn't come around the first year because he didn't want to be part of it, but we finally got him to do the things he liked to do like the Senior Tackle and come over to practice.

He would call me and say, "Are you practicing for Michigan?" I said, "Oh God, coach. I'm practicing for Michigan State right now. I've got my hands full." He'd say, "You better forget about them and prepare for Michigan." He was always supportive of me. I don't think they would have fired me in 1987 if Woody had been alive. He died earlier that year.

~ From Pete Carroll ~

I had worked with him the year before too, so I was already in tune with his classic old-school work ethic and mentality. Tough, physical, drive people and hard-charging. High expectations. That's what Earle was. He'd come out of Woody's program and was a disciple. Nobody's Woody but he operated in the same vein and style and it was very successful because he was very consistent and a very smart guy.

Earle added to that style of coaching that I'd been around most of my career. He added to the importance of fundamentals and that the heartbeat of the game was about running the football and playing tough defense.

CHAPTER 4

On Coaching

"Leaders are made. They are not born, and they are made just like anything else has ever been made in this country—by hard effort. And that's the price that we all have to pay to achieve that goal or any goal.

"And despite what we say about being born equal, none of us really are born equal, but rather unequal. And yet the talented are no more responsible for their birthright than the underprivileged. And the measure of each should be what each does in a specific situation."

—Vince Lombardi

Wayne Woodrow Hayes was the head football coach of the Ohio State University for 28 years and has 205 victories to his credit. Football coaches love summer—the preparation time for games to come—and Coach Hayes was no exception to the rule. Coach Hayes had some great sayings for this period, such as: "You win with people . . . You win with good people." In recruiting he would say, "The woods are full of good kids. Get me the good football players." The one I remember most is: "He's a better football player than he thinks he is—our job is to get him to play to his ability and sometimes better than his ability." Coach Hayes worked us all like dogs during two-a-days. He was truly a dedicated coach and a great leader of young men.

> *"A team doesn't stay the same, it is either getting better or getting worse, and you want to be sure your team is getting better."*

> *"Look for mistakes made by your team, and if they are taking coaching, the mistakes are less frequent and not always the same mistakes."*

> *"Always take action to improve your team."*

> *"In November is when the contenders rise to the top and the pretenders fall by the wayside."*

> *"During the month of November in Big Ten football, the big rivalry games take place and the weather changes. Weather and field conditions are sometimes bad and must be considered in planning. "*

> *"Cover all situations, practice so in the game you overcome all the adversities."*

> *"The best prepared football team will be the winner in the big games."*

> *"In November, you must be the coach that makes each player think he is a little better than he thinks he is."*

Good coaching is winning the game.

Good coaching is having your team ready to play every Saturday.

Good coaching is great play selection and defense selection.

Good coaching is having each player performing to his ability or above.

Good coaching is seeing your team perform the fundamentals of football—blocking, tackling, running, and catching—to great heights.

Good coaching is outperforming your opponents on offense, defense, and special teams.

Good coaching is overcoming adversity during the game.

Good coaching is good halftime adjustments.

Good coaching is finding a way to win.

Remember: Players play the game—coaches coach the game.

Every year before the start of the Big Ten season, I read a letter from a prominent Ohio State alumnus. It says:

> *"Dear Coach Bruce: In all fairness to you and your family we feel the following advice should not be taken lightly. As you know, Columbus is the graveyard of coaches.*
>
> *Form no lasting friendships.*
>
> *Never, never, never lose to Michigan, and if you do lose, three times and you're out.*
>
> *Don't buy a home.*
>
> *Do not argue religion or politics (there are plenty of other ways to get fired without adding to the list.)*
>
> *Always agree with the president, athletic director, trustees, sports writers, and big money men downtown. In other words, be wishy-washy.*
>
> *Always have a strong guard on the bench facing the stands (those attacks from the rear can be disastrous).*
>
> *Keep your business matters fluid.*
>
> *Stay away from barber shops in season (get your wife to cut your hair, she will be doing it sooner or later).*
>
> *Run like hell for the dressing room after a losing game."*

The first football game I ever attended in the "Horseshoe" was the Missouri Tigers vs. Ohio State in September of 1949. We won that day 35-34. As all freshmen were ineligible to play, I was in the stands. I will never forget the band coming out of the tunnel onto the field, the drum major throwing the baton over the crossbar of the goalposts and catching it, and the enthusiasm of the fans–it made the hair on the back of my neck stick up. I became a Buckeye for life that day.

The Missouri game always brings to mind a coaching story. When coach Wes Fesler left Ohio State after the Snow Bowl game of 1950, former Missouri coach Don Faurot was hired as head coach of the Buckeyes–for one day. After accepting the job in Columbus, Coach Faurot returned to Missouri to discuss the decision with Mrs. Faurot. They decided that the high pressure and win-win attitude of Buckeyes football was too much for them. As a result of that decision, OSU got Woody and Ann Hayes instead. They thrived on the pressure and win-win attitude for twenty-eight years. Woody and Ann Hayes were truly two of a kind.

Every time Ohio State plays Illinois, it brings back memories of Woody Hayes and his history lesson on Honest Abe Lincoln. Woody's lecture about the 16th president of the United States included that, at 6'4", 180 pounds, Abe could have been a great offensive tackle or tight end, but not a good football coach.

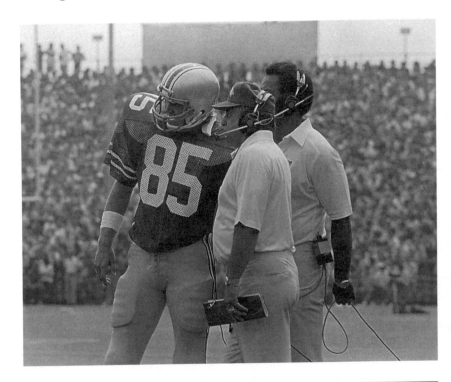

Woody Hayes said many times that the defense keys the upset win, normally with a shutout. Woody said that great defensive teams are always high spirited and show their morale by their speed to the ball, called pursuit, so that one or two missed tackles will not result in a long touchdown run. Coach Hayes had a few thoughts on building a strong defense.

Protect the open side of the field, so as to stop long runs and passes. Even place an extra player to the open side.

Place personnel on the defense—flop personnel—so the talents of the individual player fit the defensive philosophy.

You must always take away an opponent's best play and thereby reduce the effectiveness of their best player.

Always take away the great running back or quarterback— make them beat you left-handed.

Avoid defensive penalties. Defensive penalties (face mask, holding, pass interference, late hits, etc.) allow the opponent to keep the ball.

Paint a clear, vivid picture so players can see the "big play" and make "big plays." Show them on film. Ready them mentally and physically to make great plays.

"They may beat us by outcoaching me. But I resolved a long time ago that nobody would ever beat me by outworking me."

—W. W. Hayes

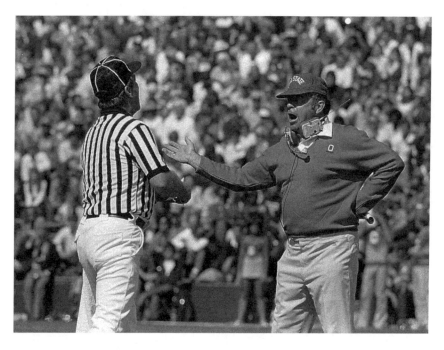

"The best kind of leadership is not that which is spoken, or even leadership by actions. The best type of leadership is that which comes from your heart and soul."

—Kirk Lowdermilk, former OSU football player,
professional football player

Coaching is very important to winning in college football. Successful college coaching consists of many important factors: recruiting good players and students; preparing your team in the fundamentals of the game and the strategy and tactics of winning football; personal touches with the players, fans, and professors; running a "clean" program under the NCAA rules.

The scoreboard is the judge of a good coach. More wins than losses will usually keep you coaching at your college or university. There are definitely more good football coaches than there are good football programs.

There are two types of coaches. Maintenance coaches must keep up the strong football program and winning tradition. The builders take a losing program and make it a winner. I like builders, like Coach Tiller at Purdue, Coach Snyder at Kansas State, Coach Bowden at Florida State, and Coach Spurrier at Florida.

Coaching is not only an art, it is a science.

~ My coaches ~

I was blessed to work with some amazing coaches, many of whom have gone on to reach the pinnacle in the coaching profession. Here are some thoughts on a few of them:

*   *   *

About Pete Carroll

I hired Pete on my Iowa State staff in 1978 and then had him come with me when I took over Ohio State the next year. He's got a real different background. He went to the University of Pacific in Stockton, Calif. I had no idea what kind of town Stockton was. I looked it up and started reading about it and boy is that a tough town. A really tough town.

He was a great guy, and a great person to have on my staff. He had a lot of energy. He was a young, enthusiastic coach—very good with kids. He was all you want in an assistant football coach.

Pete is an excitable coach even now, so you can imagine what he was like when he was with me when he wasn't even 30. In '79, we were up at Minnesota and they were ahead of us 19-7 at halftime. He comes down from the press box and says, "You're on your own! We can't stop them! You're on your own! We can't stop them!"

I knew I had to get the coaches calmed down before I talked to the team. So I said to the whole defensive staff, "Keep your mouth shut. Don't you open your mouths. I'll talk to the team at halftime and lay out the picture of how we're going to win the second half."

Sometimes, the best defense is a good offense so I told them the way to come back was to keep the ball and keep their offense off the field. And we did. We won 22-19. It took quite an effort from my players, and three of them ended up laying on the grass with concussions. I knew they weren't right because they were eating the grass.

* * *

About Nick Saban

Pete Carroll took the job to become defensive coordinator at North Carolina State before the Rose Bowl when we played USC. I didn't take Pete with us to California because I knew his heart would be with his new job and I thought it'd be better for him to get started there. To replace him, I took a young coach named Nick Saban. He was real close with Denny Fryzel, who took over the University of Tampa job when I left for Iowa State.

Nick was a very good teacher and very well-organized. He was very knowledgeable about pass defense and defense in general. That was his forte. I had him for two years, and he did an outstanding job. He was a great recruiter, too. He's very articulate. He knew how to warm them up.

He had a different personality. He's very close-lipped. He didn't say much. But what he said, you better listen to.

* * *

About Urban Meyer

Urban started at Ohio State as a graduate assistant. I told Tom Lichtenberg, who was in charge of our GA program, to go out and get the two best graduate assistants you can possibly get. No one could have a better coach than Tom Lichtenberg. One of the guys he hired was Urban. He was working at St. Xavier High School in Cincinnati as a volunteer assistant after graduating from UC.

Urban tells the story of me chewing his ass about the first drill he set up. It was a cone drill and the cones weren't anywhere where they should have been, to me at least. I said, "Can't you do that?!"

But he caught on quick. He caught on very quick. You didn't have to tell him two times how to do something. He could think for himself and he got some good advice from people around him. I had good coaches. I had really good coaches.

Urban was here in 1986-87 at a tough time. I got fired in 1987 and he ended up at Illinois State with Jim Heacock—a very nice guy and very thorough football coach. Jim became the longtime defensive coordinator under Jim Tressel with the Buckeyes. But when Jim was at Illinois State, I coached against him when I was at Northern Iowa. After Ohio State, I ended up at Colorado State, where Lou Holtz's son Skip was one of my assistants. I'd wanted to keep Skip for two years but after one season, his dad called and said he needed Skip back. So I needed a receivers coach and I interviewed Urban. He was by far the most thorough coach I interviewed. He was there for three years for me before I was fired. He had a great mind and was a great recruiter.

When I was at Colorado State, the first kid I recruited was a player named Billy Gonzales. He had some issues and I told Urban, "You get that kid straightened out. You and (wife) Shelley spend time with him. If you spend time with him, you can straighten him around, because he's just had a bad start in life." They did straighten him out. They kept him busy, showed an interest in him, in his academics. Urban did a great job.

*   *   *

Meyer and Bowling Green

Urban then went to Notre Dame. One day in 2000, I got a call from Bob Sebo, my great friend from Salem, Ohio. He was a Bowling Green alumnus and he said that they needed a head football coach. He asked if I knew anybody. I said, "I sure do. You go get Urban Meyer from Notre Dame. Take him, and he'll be the greatest coach you've ever had. He'll make you win right away because he's a good recruiter, a good coach, a good communicator. He'll be able to do everything that program needs to be established and that's to get the kids to stay for the games and promote the games and do all that. Well, they took him."

The rest is history.

* * *

About Woody Hayes

The biggest things I learned from Woody were the importance of toughness and discipline. Not making mistakes, no fumbles, no interceptions, not going offsides. If you master that and don't make mistakes that beat you, you have a very good chance to win. Teaching how to tackle, how to block, he was very sound at that. He was very good at motivating players. He worked a lot with individual motivation. When it came to big games, everybody understood what their role was in the game.

He did a really good job of being with the players when they needed a boost and what they could do to help win the game.

* * *

Woody and Bo

Woody normally did a great job motivating the team for Michigan. The one time he faltered was in Bo's first year in 1969. He didn't give Bo enough credit. He didn't realize until after the game what they did to prepare for us.

When Bo took the Michigan job, Woody was a little shaken. Bo played for Woody. Bo coached for Woody. Bo was fired every week by Woody, which was part of the deal when you worked for Woody. I found out that when he got to Michigan, Bo himself was very much like Woody. I heard that Bo fired his coaches every week. That's what his assistant coaches would tell you.

Anyway, in '69, Michigan was really motivated because the year before, we went for 2 at the end of a 50-14 win. There was a lot of confusion on that play. The guy who yelled to go for 2 was our great fullback, Jim Otis. He was the one who started yelling, "Go for 2, go for 2!"

But then Woody was asked after the game, "Why did you go for 2?" and he said, "Because I couldn't go for 3." I thought it was very clever, but I didn't think it was very smart. They were very prepared for us in '69 when we were No. 1 and undefeated. Everything we did, they had figured. They stopped the one pattern— the jet pattern to Bruce Jankowski -- that was our bread and butter. Our assistant coach Hugh Hindman was yelling from the beginning, 'Don't throw that pass, Woody!"

I got a little wind of what we were in for before the start of the game. To get up to the press box, you had to walk through the stands. I was walking up and about the 17th row a guy grabs me and shakes me and says, "You're going to get yours today, buster. You're going to get yours today." Then I got to about the 30th row and another guy jumps out and grabs me today and says, "It's all over today, It's all over today." I thought, 'Holy crap, they're worked up.' Then somehow, we went to the wrong end of the field, and they snowballed us all the way up to get to our side of the field.

We lost 24-12 and I don't even remember the drive back from Ann Arbor. Woody was in denial, like it didn't happen. It happened. I didn't think it could ever happen to us with as great as that '69 team was. That made him fearful of Bo forever after.

Minnesota

In 1966, I was the assistant in charge of special teams. That year we played at Minnesota. With about 13 minutes to go, we trailed 14-0 before scoring a touchdown. The Golden Gophers then played at old Memorial Stadium in Minneapolis. The stadium back then didn't have digital clocks. Instead, it had the old-fashioned winding clock, and it was hard to tell exactly how much time was left. That must have confused Woody because he insisted on attempting an onside kick. We called that onside-kick unit the kangaroo squad after the way the ball is supposed to bounce on that kick.

I was on the sideline and the coaches upstairs who were hearing Woody say, "Get the kangaroo team," are telling me, "Get away from him! Get away from him!" They're thinking that if Woody can't find me to tell me to get the kangaroo team on the field, they might dodge that bullet. So I'm starting to move away from Woody when something hits me in the middle of my back. I go forward and then come back and look up and there's Woody. He said, "I WANT THE KANGAROO." So I said to the guys upstairs, "He's going to get the kangaroo. If you don't want the kangaroo, you better come down and stop it because I'm getting the kangaroo right now." I went and got the kangaroo unit. Sure enough, the kick failed. Minnesota got the ball at the 50-yard line and drove down to kick a field goal. We lost 17-7.

Woody walks in to the locker room after the game and he is steaming. They had a wall that was being fixed and had plywood in its place. Woody put his fist right through the plywood, all the way through. We all looked it, the kids looked at it, like, "Oh my God!" All the coaches were standing back in the shower watching from the shower. We didn't want to get near him.

The next time we came up there two years later, the hole was still there. The new guys were like, "He did that?!" That was Minnesota. I learned one thing – knowing the time on the clock is very important. I still can't believe he put his arm through there.

"To be a dedicated coach, player, student, father, or brother is a full-time responsibility. Dedication is taking it far beyond the two-hour workout or sending a card on someone's birthday. Being dedicated to a person, job, or any cause is far different than spending time or just caring about it.

When your actions reflect spending most of your waking hours thinking of ways to improve and working hard to be the best, this is true dedication. Because of our limitation on time and energy, it is difficult to be completely dedicated to a large number of endeavors."

—Urban Meyer, head coach, Ohio State University,
and Earle Bruce's former graduate assistant at OSU
and wide receivers coach at Colorado State

What is great coaching? It is setting a good example for the players, teaching them good football and good habits. Treat players as you would treat your own sons.

Coaching football is a great profession. I enjoyed coaching for forty-three years. I worked hard, but always enjoyed myself. I could honestly say I never worked a day in my life.

A successful coach is a good teacher. Teach the fundamentals of football, teach the players to work hard and give their best effort, teach a good team attitude, teach discipline.

To be a successful coach you must see that players graduate. The coach is a role model on and off the field, and he must help the players to learn what he himself has learned from playing the game of football.

In coaching football, it is important to remember:

Players do what they are coached to do.

The best-coached team is going to win.

Be sure and recognize winners and play them.

Winners have intensity.

Praise or criticize the act—not the player.

Cover all facets of the game in your coaching so as to give your team and players the edge.

Confidence is the name of the game. When players think they can—they can! You must know the players and what they can do.

Coaches must teach mental and physical toughness so that if a player gets knocked down, he can get up and go again.

Coaching is being positive, honest, organized, determined. It is being yourself, taking criticism, and being second guessed. And you must love your players and want to see them succeed.

No head college football coach likes to see upperclassmen in summer school for eligibility purposes. Coach Hayes used to say, "discipline is 90% anticipation," so always prevent the problems by seeing that a young player is at study table getting the necessary tutoring, and be sure and monitor class attendance. Coach Hayes also said that if you recruited a young man to Ohio State for football, you should see that he graduates. Don't give the player a chance to goof up. Failure to attend class is inexcusable, immature, and the sign of a very negative attitude. This attitude must change to a positive, mature attitude for the man to be successful in life. Someone must ensure that the young man's direction changes so that his attitude works for him rather than against him. That someone could be his football coach, friend, and/or family member.

It's great to have success on the football field, but if you ask me, it is much better to have success and a great life off the football field.

~ The best place to learn ~

The best way to learn to coach is to go be a high-school coach. High-school coaching will teach you more than anything. It's dealing with the people, dealing with the discipline of that. Some didn't want to go that way but I still feel that way. That's because I did that. I think graduate assistants become too football-oriented. They don't think about the other things with the kid. The greatest thing in the world is having a relationship with a young man and he's a better person because of how you've coached him. He becomes a good man in town, and you've instilled some things into him that are good qualities.

In the fall of 1983, I attended a high school football game in Ohio to observe a great young prospect for Ohio State football. He was a linebacker, tailback, punter, punt returner, and sold popcorn before the game. He played so well in the game that I thought it might be a one-game effort. So I returned the following week to observe him again and he did the same spectacular things. He played better than any high school football player I had ever seen, and I had coached high school football for thirteen years and had seen a lot of great high school football players.

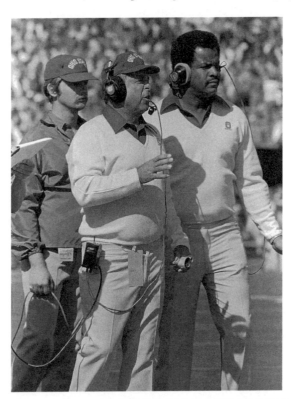

Chris Spielman signed to attend Ohio State in the fall of 1984. He wanted to start for the Buckeyes as a freshman. He asked and was given a big "OK" to play in the Ohio All-Star game in July in Stark County. Because of a sprained ankle from the All-Star game, Chris did not start the first game versus Oregon State. It was too much for him. He could not handle the bench. Before halftime, with OSU behind 13-6, I heard behind me a chant of "I've got to play, I've got to play." It was the stomping, pacing Chris Spielman. I nudged defensive coordinator Bob Tucker and asked, "When are you going to play Chris?" He looked at me in dismay and said that Chris was injured and only a freshman. With Oregon State winning, he didn't know whether Chris was ready. I said, "He's ready!" The half ended with Oregon State ahead 13-7.

At halftime I ordered Bob Tucker to start Chris. It meant benching Pepper Johnson, as they were both playing the same inside linebacker position. Reluctantly Bob said yes. Chris made the first ten tackles of the second half, running over, around, and through the blockers to do it. We went on to win the game, and the next week, both Pepper and Chris were starters.

Chris Spielman is a quality young man and a great football player. Eight years with the Detroit Lions made him a leading tackler and a tough player. In his second year with the Buffalo Bills he was temporarily sidelined with a serious injury. Whether he plays, coaches, or just inspires people, he will always have something to do with the game of football, because he loves it.

Note: Chris retired in 1999 and is now a college football analyst for ESPN. I say God bless the doers of the world and God bless Chris Spielman—he is a doer.

"In the relationship with players, the essence of coaching is the combination of being a teacher and parent. It is helping a player reach his goal in athletics and life. More so, it's challenging a player beyond that to continually improve and grow toward reaching his full potential. My coaching mentors have taught me that this situation is best achieved through individual attention to the player both on and off the field. An old coaching axiom says, 'They don't care how much you know, until they know how much you care.'"

—Bob Tucker, former OSU
assistant football coach

~ Tradition ~

The best college football programs have traditions which separate them from the rest. The Ohio State Buckeyes have such traditions. Most of them help to create our winning program.

The Ohio State Marching Band, with Script Ohio, the dotting of the "i", the coming out of the tunnel, "Hang on Sloopy," and the great drum majors.

The "gold pants" award for a victory over Michigan, initiated thanks to Coach Frances Schmidt's statement that "Michigan players, like Ohio State players, put their pants on one leg at a time."

The Captains' Brunch following the homecoming game. The great elite leaders of the Buckeyes meet on Sunday at noon.

Buckeye Grove, where the All-American OSU players are honored with a Buckeye tree.

The Victory Bell in the southeast tower of the "Horseshoe" tolls after every home victory.

The Friday night meal at the OSU golf course, with steak, pecan rolls, and all the trimmings.

The Stadium, the "Horseshoe"—what a place to play your games. The sellouts and enthusiasm of students and alumni for the team.

The Big Ten Conference and the Rose Bowl.

The Big Game—the Michigan game—a great rivalry.

Strong football traditions mean strong football players and a greater opportunity to win games.

"*As a coach, it is important to emphasize the following to your players: Forget about yourself. Remember, less me and more we. Don't be concerned with who gets the credit. Always do your best. Do more than what others expect. Expect more than what is possible. Never feel sorry for yourself. Remember it is a privilege to be a member of a team. Find a way to lead in some way. Be willing to pay the price it takes for success. Have class. Never build yourself up by tearing others down. Be committed.*

"*The above are qualities of teamwork. Being unselfish is often a rare trait in our society, but a good coach can find or cultivate this attitude in his players. Ultimately, then, they will strive to make their team, not themselves, the priority.*"

—Tom Lichtenberg, former OSU assistant football coach

~ Coaching ~

What is good coaching?

A good coach has a sound technical knowledge of the game of football and an insight into athletes, which he incorporates into a highly organized twelve-month coaching plan.

A good coach is capable of helping the student perform up to his athletic ability.

A good coach builds his team on a foundation of individual skill coaching.

A good coach keeps abreast of technical and scientific advances by being actively involved in the physical education profession.

A good coach is capable of adjusting his game to fit his players' intellectual and neuromuscular skill levels.

A good coach applies scientific principles of conditioning on a twelve-month basis. He knows that the extra strength, flexibility, and skill developed in the off-season can spell the difference between a winner and a loser.

A good coach emphasizes education first and football second.

A good coach hates to lose, but he won't try to win at any cost.

A good coach teaches the long-range values of football participation and is aware of the relationship between the abstractions within value theory and winning ball games. He is aware of this relationship, and uses it to motivate the student-athlete.

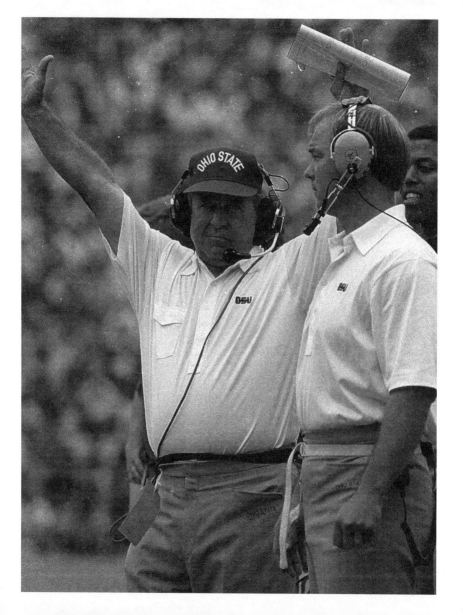

~ The Coach ~

Who loses the important game? The Coach
Who has to shoulder all the blame? The Coach
Who, to teach boys to play, is hired?
And yet if one of them grows tired
And fails to score is promptly fired?
The Coach

Who character is asked to build? The Coach
With customers, to keep the stadium filled? The Coach
Who plans formations, old and new,
And tells youngsters what to do,
But if they can't, is told "you're through."
The Coach

Who by the thousands, second guessed? The Coach
Is jeered for plays he thought were best? The Coach
Who has my deepest sympathy?
Who is it I'd not care to be,
Regardless of salary?
The Coach

—Edgar Guest

Michigan game, 1987

When I was a young lad, I remember President Franklin D. Roosevelt saying that December 7, 1941—the day the Japanese bombed Pearl Harbor—was a day of infamy, a day to remember. My day of infamy is November 17, 1987, the day I was fired from Ohio State. The Monday of Michigan Week. What timing. You can't imagine the feeling. It's like getting kicked in the breadbasket by a hundred mules.

You might think that my first thought would be to quit and not do anything, but my time in football has taught me that when you get hit hard or knocked down, you get up and go again. You fight for what's right. You put personal things aside and concentrate on the objective—beat Michigan. The players were great, and I mean really great. We stopped talking about the firing and talked about the most important game in football—the Michigan game. The game preparation and the trip to Michigan went well. The exception was the start of the game. We started cold and very slow and hesitant. Michigan's Jamie Morris had 15 carries and 112 yards, and Mike Gillette kicked 2 field goals for 13 points to lead in the 2nd quarter. Tom Tupa's 4-yard pass to Everett Ross made it a 13-7 halftime score.

One of the keys for the Michigan game is for every player to play hard, never give up, hit, and tackle.

Oh! What a great Buckeye second half—the Bucks would not be denied.

A short five-yard pass from Tom Tupa to Carlos Snow ended in a seventy-yard touchdown, and the extra point made it 14-13 Ohio State. An interception by David Brown put the ball within scoring range on the Michigan 19. Another pass from Tom Tupa to Vince Workman to the one-yard line, followed by a quarterback sneak for the touchdown and a missed extra point, left the score 20-13 Ohio State. A twenty-six-yard field goal by Frantz made the score 23-20 in the 4th quarter.

The defense gave up seven points in the 3rd quarter and shut out Michigan in the 4th quarter. Great defense in the second half—Chris Spielman, sixteen tackles; David Brown, eight tackles, one interception; Derek Eisman, seven tackles; Ray Jackson, eight tackles; Mike McCray, seven tackles; Mike Showalter, four tackles, two quarterback sacks.

Michigan is still the "Big One," the Big Game. Never, never, never give up or accept defeat in this game. Make your plays, give your greatest effort, and you will win the Michigan game.

CHAPTER 5

On Success

"We must be physically and mentally fit because the times demand that we not only compete, but that we excel, and we must do it with enthusiasm, the enthusiasm found more prominently on the field of sport."

—President Gerald R. Ford

~ The Man in the Arena ~

The 26th president of the United States, Theodore Roosevelt, was a tough, energetic, daring, and fearless young leader of the country. "Teddy" led the charge at San Juan in Cuba during the Spanish-American War. He was a real "Rough Rider." He believed in going hard at everything. Teddy Roosevelt is credited with saving the game of football at the turn of the century by helping to establish rules to protect football players from injury. There had been too many deaths in the game for it to continue as it was. I remember his greatest statement concerning the game of football. It's called "The Man in the Arena."

> It's not the critic that counts,
>
> not the one who points out how the strong man stumbled
>
> or how the doer of deeds might have done them better;
>
> the credit belongs to the man who is actually in the arena,
>
> whose face is marred with sweat and dust and blood,
>
> who strives valiantly,
>
> who errors and comes up short again and again,
>
> who knows enthusiasm and great devotion and spends
>
> himself in a worthy cause.
>
> Who if he wins, knows the triumph of high achievement and
>
> who if he fails at least fails while daring greatly
>
> so that his place shall never be with the cold and timid souls
>
> who know neither victory or defeat.

~ Competition ~

On a football team, it's great to have outstanding personnel at all positions. If you have two or three people competing for playing time at each position, the competition helps improve the players. Competition is someone setting a standard for you—working hard, giving great effort, improving your athletic talent, getting better every practice and every game. Each player must be challenged by another to improve his performance. It's always an incentive to have someone issuing you a challenge to improve your performance and compete for victory. I remember the words of Jack Nicklaus: "The tougher and closer the competition, the more I enjoy golf. The golf I like or enjoy is battling shot by shot right down to the wires."

The better the competition, the better great athletes perform. The best competitors I have known react to tough competition in practice and in the championship game. There is nothing as rewarding as winning a tough game. Lack of competition is detrimental to team and individual improvement. But remember, not everyone is a competitor. Some are front-runners who, when challenged, go backward instead of forward. God bless the great competitors I have had the privilege of coaching.

~ Players ~

It is always helpful to have talented football players who are big, fast, and strong. But when I think of the qualities possessed by the great players whom I have coached, I think of the following:

Intelligent. It's easy to communicate with someone who can understand what you say, someone who has the capacity to learn, to study, to act, to dissect the game of football and college life.

Tough. A player who likes to hit and be hit. One who, when knocked down, jumps up and goes again. One who will always be ready for the big game (which is normally the next game).

Hard working. Is willing to do whatever it takes to win the championship, improve on his shortcomings, and continue to develop his best areas. Gives great effort all the time.

Positive. He believes that he and his team are number one. When that four-foot putt comes for the championship, he knows he can make it.

Dependable. Is ready five minutes before time, always ahead of everyone and already doing his assigned job.

Ambitious. He strives to get ahead and is always looking to do more than his fair share.

Championships are won with players with these qualities, not just with talented football players.

"I'll be honest, I've been blessed with some God-given ability . . . but on 4th and one, it doesn't come down to ability. It comes down to coaching, preparation, and desire."

—Jim Lachey, former OSU & professional football player

An old football player was once asked the secret of his success. He replied that it could be summed up in three words—"And Then Some."

"I discovered at an early age," he declared, "that most of the difference between average people and the top people could be explained in three words. The top layer did what was expected of them

. . . and then some.

They were thoughtful of others; they were considerate and kind, good teammates

. . . and then some.

They could be counted on in an emergency and in tough times

. . . and then some.

I am thankful for people like that for they make the World more livable, for their spirit of service and teamwork is summed up in the three little words

. . . and then some.

Sear them in your soul and brand them on your brain

. . . and then some.

Esprit de corps is the one quality above all others that distinguishes a successful team or organization from a mere aggregation of men. It is the pride in group standards and achievements which makes for the highest standards of accomplishment. Esprit means spirit, ardor, or enthusiasm, and it pertains to the individual and the group. It represents the sum total of all the forces that make for cohesion, for sticking together, and for organized willing endeavor. Esprit de corps is the sense of strength and pride that comes from being part of a distinguished and efficient organization. (The Buckeyes football team and the Ohio State Marching Band are the greatest examples of esprit de corps that Earle Bruce has ever seen.)

A young Buckeye football player in his late teens sat musing one day on the banks of the Olentangy River. A young preacher chanced to pass that way and the young man said to him, "Good Father, what shall I do to succeed in football, to win the Big Ten Championship?" The preacher answered, "Follow me," and he waded forthwith into the deepest part of the Olentangy. The water grew deeper and deeper, but the preacher led on and the boy followed until the water reached his chin. As he turned to go back, the preacher seized him by the hair of his head and held him at arm's length under the water with all his strength. Finally, when it seemed he would drown, with a mighty effort he broke away and made his way to shore. After the player ceased gasping, the preacher said to him, "Young man, what did you most want while you were held under the water?" "Air, air," the player replied. Then the preacher said, "Young man, when you desire the Big Ten title as much and are willing to fight for it as hard as you fought for air, nothing can keep you from the Big Ten Championship."

"Discipline comes from the desire to be a better player, defining a plan to get you there, and the execution of that plan. This will take a great deal of sacrifice and hard work. The complete football player is one who disciplines himself both mentally and physically."

—Mike Gimenez,
former college quarterback,
high school football coach

There are three kinds of people on every team. There are rowboat people, sailboat people, and steamboat people.

Rowboat people need to be pushed or shoved along.

Sailboat people move when a favorable wind is blowing.

Steamboat people move continuously, through calm or storm. They are the masters of themselves, their surroundings, and their fate.

God bless the steamboat people . . . they mean the most to every organization.

"*It is essential to always be willing to go where the opponent is unwilling or unable to go. This attitude must be maintained every day, all day and in every situation. Never compromise your standards.*"

—Chris Spielman,
former OSU linebacker,
professional football player

November is the stretch drive in the college football season. It is the month of almost all of the great rivalries in college football. It is the time to double your effort and fight hard.

My Buckeyes, when the fight is the grimmest,
And it seems that you cannot gain,
And you've hurtled yourself at the steel-like line,
Again and again and again.
And the tackle rebuffs your plunges,
And the ends are as swift as light,
And you've started to doubt your power,
Right then is the time to fight.

You feel that you're shot to pieces
Ah, Bucks, but some day you'll know
That the battles of life and football
Are won by the final blow.
For the ones who have hit you the hardest
Are weakened, my man, as you,
And the fight must come down to courage
The last vital drop or two.

So Buck up you heart, dear Buckeye
And though all the heavens may fall,
Give them your heart core wallop,
The weakest, yet best of all,
And I'll tell you dear Buckeye, the heroes
Who watch from their heights will say,
There's a man with the last punch of courage,
Make way for the Buckeye,
Make way for the great Buckeyes,
Make way.

November is for the contenders—not the pretenders.

The game that makes or breaks the season is the Michigan game. The Rose Bowl or Fiesta Bowl usually hang in the balance and anything less is the Toilet Bowl.

What leads the Bucks to a Michigan victory? Many things, but here are just a few to think about:

No coaching errors, or at least kept to a minimum. Pressure is a factor in this game and how the coaching staff performs on Michigan day is important.

All the Buckeyes players must turn it up a notch for victory. This is really the "Big One," and victory must not get away.

The trenches must play super. Special teams must help win the battle.

No turnovers. No major penalties. Capitalize on the opponent's turnovers.

The strongest Buckeyes players must play their best against Michigan.

All great games are won in the fourth quarter with great effort and a "goose egg" for the Wolverines.

A player's attitude must be outstanding on this day. Play hard on every play—there can be no relaxing. Every player must believe he is going to win and accept nothing less than victory.

Success is to be measured not so much by the position one has reached in life as by the obstacles which one has overcome while trying to succeed.

The measure of success is not whether you have a tough problem to deal with, but whether it's the same problem you had last year.

The secret of success is consistency of purpose. Doing little things with a great desire to please God makes them really great.

Michigan game, 1984

In 1984, with the score Ohio State 7, Michigan 6, Ohio State scored 14 points in the 4th quarter to win the game 21-6. It was a great 4th quarter victory for the Buckeyes. Turnovers in the 4th quarter—Michigan with one and Ohio State with none—made a difference in the outcome. Keith Byars led all rushers with about 100 yards and Mike Tomczak was 11 of 15 with 139 yards and no interceptions. I told Mike Lanese that he may be remembered as a Rhodes Scholar at Ohio State, but I will always remember him for the great catch on 3rd down and twelve at the Ohio State forty-three-yard line for seventeen yards, and a 1st down to keep the drive alive for the touchdown, making the score 14-6.

Very seldom do you win this game kicking field goals. So strong red-zone offense and goal-line defense usually result in winning the "Big Game." Tom Tupa had a forty-five-yard punting average and OSU's special teams played very well. Again, the defense was great, led by middle guard Larry Kolic (twelve tackles), linebacker Byron Lee (ten tackles), Pepper Johnson, S. Gordon, Dave Morrill, and Chris Spielman (all with nine tackles). The defense was swarming to the ball.

The Michigan game is by far the cleanest, least penalized, hardest fought game every season, and winning brings great rewards for the victors.

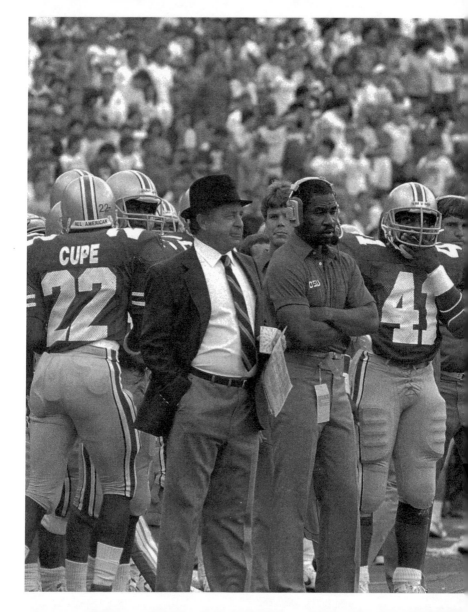

CHAPTER 6

On Teamwork

"*I believe that football instills into many men the feeling that victory comes through hard work, team play, self confidence, and an enthusiasm that amounts to dedication.*"

—President Dwight D. Eisenhower

Let's talk about the most important segment on the football team— the offensive line. The skills or techniques one needs to be a good offensive lineman are numerous and very difficult to master in a short time. If you want or need to run the football, the offensive line must get movement at the point of attack and also cut off the pursuit from the backside of the defense. The line must also protect the quarterback from being rushed or sacked; you must keep the defense out of the face of the quarterback so he can throw the ball effectively. Don't let the quarterback get hit! The big offensive lineman must be mobile, hostile, have great arm strength, good size, and be in great overall condition so as to be able to play four quarters of football. The offensive line gets very little credit (except at OSU) for a job well done but a lot of criticism for a poor job. Offensive success in a game can be measured by total yards rushing, rushing touchdowns in the red zone, number of quarterback sacks given up, short yardage conversion percentage, etc. Size is very important for a lineman, but toughness is more important. Smart, hard workers are equally important. The offensive line is special to me.

Let's talk about the most important segment on the football team—the defensive backfield. Its primary job is to prevent the long pass or the long run. A good defensive back must be a sure tackler, must be able to run backward faster than a receiver can run forward, cannot blow pass coverages, must have good hands to intercept passes, and must have speed to return interceptions. You look great as a defensive back when you do everything right, but when the opponent throws one over your head for a touchdown, you look like a stooge. Ohio State has been blessed with great defensive backs and great secondary coaching. The defensive backs have covered receivers well, they break on the ball well, tackle well, and demonstrate an "I like football" attitude. Good defensive backs ensure that a defense can take chances, because you can play receivers man-to-man or disguise it well and play zone. With great speed in the secondary, you won't give up the big play.

The defensive secondary must play as a unit against the run and the pass. God bless good pass coverage and big plays by the defensive backs.

Let's talk about the most important segment on the football team—the defensive line. We talk about skilled players (quarterbacks, running backs, wide receivers) as being important and talented. But the defensive line must be big, fast, quick, and tough, and must react very quickly to either run or pass. They must never get blocked or knocked down. They must play their position, then pursue the ball with reckless abandon. They must be able to disengage from a block and tackle a big, fast running back, or put pressure on, or sack the quarterback. They must be in great condition to stay big and play such a fatiguing position. Yes, the defensive line is the most important segment on the football team, and we need not only one, but sometimes four or five of them!

Let's talk about the most important position on the football team—linebacker. What position on the defense must demonstrate that great leadership brings great victories? The linebacker must support the run first, but also help in pass defense, either underneath in zone pass defense or with the tight ends or backs in man-to-man. This position should lead the defensive team in tackles and big plays in almost every game while demonstrating confidence, toughness, leadership, and courage. The people playing this position should have size, speed, and the ability to read on the move, and must never get blocked, knocked down, or faked out. The linebacker must not only be a shock trooper but also a storm trooper. He can be the buffer between the coaches and the players.

Let's talk about the most important position on the football team—running back. What position needs great athletes with speed, agility, and a sense of direction? The running back must run north and south to gain yards for the offense. He must be someone who, when knocked to the ground, can get up and go again and again. He must always protect the ball, so as to not fumble. He must have great hands so as to catch pitches and passes. He must be elusive, but also have the ability to lower his shoulder and get a few more yards. This is the running back position. A major college football power should always have a pair and a spare. The Buckeyes are usually blessed with a pair and two spares.

What is the most important segment of the football team? Which segment of the team could gain or lose more yardage in one play (such as the punt, punt return, kickoff, kickoff return, extra point, and field goal) than any other segment? Yes, special teams (including the kicking game) are a very important part of the football team. The punter must master the skills of the punt—catching the center snap, dropping the ball correctly, placing the foot on the ball, and all the tactical and strategic situations connected with the actual punt—and then protect and cover the punt. The kicker must master

all the techniques of kicking—proper steps, timing, hitting the ball, follow-through and accuracy for extra points and field goals, and great distance on kickoffs. Blocking and tackling are always important on special teams. Courage is of great importance in coverage and catching the ball. Good coaching is very important for this segment of the team, and skilled punters and kickers make teaching a lot easier.

What is the most important segment of the football team? Which segment contributes the most to the success of the football team? All segments of the team are equally important to its success. The whole team is important, not just one segment. If one segment breaks down, it can be disastrous and lead to defeat, yet great plays by one segment can lead to victory. Football is the greatest team game of all. The football player must think first of how he can contribute to the success of the team rather than to his own personal success. The football player must be totally unselfish and team-oriented. "We" and "us" are foremost, and "I, me, and mine" are secondary. Performance is the cry—not the potential one possesses for the game.

The success of a football team is directly related to the success of each segment. The better each segment performs on Saturday, the greater the victory. Likewise, if one segment does not perform well, it could lead to disaster and defeat. The more fun a player has (or the more he loves the game of football), the more success he has playing the game. You are never a failure if you always give the best that you can. That is success.

The goal is for every segment to play as well as it can and contribute to the success of the team on Saturday. And success is victory.

Football is a single segment game—TEAM. The coaches' responsibility is to create and mold a coordinated efficiency out of eleven hard-driving, eager, dedicated, highly individual athletes.

Football is the greatest team game there is in sports. Why? Because there are approximately one hundred players on a team (only eleven on the field), but you must have an offensive team, defensive team, and special teams, plus people ready to play in case of injury or adversity. Players and coaches must always be on the same page and in unity with one another so as to ensure victory. You must set aside personalities and bring each player's character to the forefront for the good of the team. The eleven players on the field must play as one, yet keep their individuality for the good of the team. Team is the key word. A football team has the values of a family.

There is a law—the law of the jungle—about which Rudyard Kipling wrote:

> *Now this is the law of the jungle*
>
> *As old and as true as the sky.*
>
> *And that wolf that keeps it may prosper*
>
> *But the wolf that shall break it must die.*
>
> *As the creeper that girdles the tree trunk*
>
> *The law runneth forward and back*
>
> *And the strength of the pack is the wolf*
>
> *And the strength of the wolf is the pack.*

Remember: A team together is a winning team.

~ Cooperation ~

We can't play alone in the game of life,
We're dependent, my friend, on others,
We cannot "get by" in the struggle and strife
Except for the help of our Brothers.

> *Whatever we plan or whatever we do,*
> *Whatever we give of the best of us,*
> *Is meant to include all fellow men, too*
> *And add to the joy of the rest of us.*

Whatever we vision, whatever we dream,
Be we lofty or lowly in station.
Whatever our idea, invention or scheme,
We are working for all of Creation.

> *God is running the world and his vast universe*
> *And blesses the worst and the best of us,*
> *The gifts He has made to divinely bestow,*
> *Are not only for you, but for the rest of us.*

You may call it by this or call it by that,
Teamwork or plain Cooperation,
Together we stand, by ourselves we fall flat,
Together, my friend, we're the nation.

> *Whatever we do, whatever we plan,*
> *We can't stand alone; even the best of us*
> *Must share our gifts with our good fellow man,*
> *For we're only a part of the Rest of Us.*

—Author unknown

~ Team ~

It's all very well to have courage and skill
And it's fine to be counted a star;
But the single deed with its touch of the thrill
Doesn't tell us the man you are.
For there's no lone hand in the game we play
We must work on a bigger scheme
And the thing that counts in the world today
Is How Do You Pull With the Team?

—Author Unknown

~ Billy the Bricklayer ~

This is about courage, toughness, ambition, willingness to work, good attitude, dependability, and good communication.

Billy was a friend and a very good bricklayer. He had to file an insurance claim, and as a result received a letter from the company requesting more information about the claim.

The insurance company said in the letter that they needed more information than what Bill had answered in "Block 2" as to the cause of the injury, to which Bill had answered, "Trying to do the job alone."

Bill further explained. "I decided to finish a job on a Saturday by myself and not bring in my helpers or crew. The job was on top of a five-story building, putting a brick edge around the top of the roof. As I finished the job, I found I had five-hundred pounds of brick left over on the top of the building. Rather than carry the bricks down the stairs, I set up a pulley and filled a barrel with bricks and lowered them down the side of the building, after securing the end of the rope at ground level in preparation for lowering the bricks. I flung the bricks in the barrel (five-hundred pounds of them) out clear of the building and went down and untied the rope, holding it securely to insure the slow descent of the barrel of bricks. Please check block #6 on the questionnaire where it asks for my weight—145 pounds.

"When the barrel, on the way down, and me going up, met between the second and third floor, it was the cause of my bruises and lacerations on my back. When I reached the roof, my hand jammed into the pulley, causing the broken thumb. Even with the pain from the hand, I held the rope tightly and did not let go. The barrel hit the ground and the bottom fell out and bricks are all over. Devoid of the bricks, the barrel weighed less than fifty pounds. I again refer you to block #6, my weight—145 pounds. This caused my rapid descent, and near the second floor, I met the barrel coming up. This explains the injuries to my legs and lower back. Slowed only slightly, I landed on the pile of bricks. My back was only sprained and internal injuries were at a minimum. I lost presence of mind and let go of the rope, as you can imagine. The empty barrel crashed down on top of me. I trust this answers all of your concerns and please know that I am finished trying to do the job alone. Yours sincerely, Bill."

I submit that if each of us went off to do the job alone, we would risk facing the same results. To do the job alone means going at it alone against some very powerful opponents or adversaries. If we are to be successful in what we do, it is imperative that we work together as a team.

~ I'm Gonna Try ~

I'm gonna try to play the game,
And play it hard and play it fair.
I may not win, but just the same
I'm gonna try and do my share.

> *I may not always meet the test*
> *As well as some more clever "guy,"*
> *But while my heart beats in my chest,*
> *I'm gonna try.*

I'm gonna try to stand the gaff,
Yet keep my nerve; I'm gonna try
To love and work and play and laugh,
Never show no yellow streak.

> *I'm gonna struggle to be kind and not*
> *Grow hard of face and eye.*
> *I'll flop at times, but never mind,*
> *I'm gonna try.*

I'm gonna try to be a friend that
Folks can trust and who they know
Will be the same to the end, whether
The luck runs high or low.

> *I'll hitch my wagon to a star and*
> *Set my foal up in the sky.*
> *And though I may not get far,*
> I'm gonna try.

Michigan game, 1979

What a crowd at Michigan to watch the 1979 game. A record 106,255. Once again, outscoring Michigan 6-0 in the 4th quarter was the answer in an 18-15 victory. The Buckeyes found a way to win with a blocked punt by Jim Laughlin and a run in for a touchdown by Todd Bell.

The defense, led by linebackers Al Washington and Marcus Marek, was swarming to the ball. Ray Ellis had an important pass interception to stop a Michigan drive. Special teams made a difference, led by Valde Yanakievski with two field goals, Tom Orosz with a forty-one-yard punting average, and the blocked punt by Jim Laughlin.

The offense scored the first Ohio State touchdown against Michigan since 1975 with an eighteen-yard pass from Art Schlichter to Larry Hunter. Art was 12 for 22 with 196 yards. We used four tailbacks (Murray, Gayle, Spencer, and Johnson) because of injuries. There were 2 fullbacks, Volley and Campbell, who had 236 yards net rushing. Doug Donley had three catches for eighty-seven yards.

What a great win, Big Ten Championship, and Rose Bowl trip in 1979. Again, all the Buckeyes football players played great versus Michigan.